Be an eco hero

On the move

Sue Barraclough

W
FRANKLIN WATTS
LONDON•SYDNEY

First published in 2010
by Franklin Watts

Copyright © Franklin Watts 2010

Franklin Watts
338 Euston Road
London NW1 3BH

Franklin Watts Australia
Level 17/207 Kent Street
Sydney, NSW 2000

Series editor: Sarah Peutrill
Art director: Jonathan Hair
Design: Big Blu Design
Illustrator: Gary Swift

Dewey number: 388

ISBN 978 0 7496 9337 4

Printed in China

Franklin Watts is a division of
Hachette Children's Books, an
Hachette UK company.
www.hachette.co.uk

Credits: Ravind Balavaman/
Shutterstock: 27tr. Sarah Bossert/
Shutterstock: 15tl. Jacek Chabraszewski/
istockphoto: 15b. Chris Fairclough/
Franklin Watts: 22, 27b. Jim Fromer/
istockphoto: 9tl. Jeff Greenburg/Alamy:
21t. Kim Gunkel/istockphoto: 25bl.
Jupiter/Goodshot/Alamy: 10. Kathy
Kaplan/istockphoto: 11t. Michael Klinec/
Alamy: 23. Krzysztof Kwiafkowski /
istockphoto: 18. Gary D. Landesman/
Corbis: 16. Leontura/istockphoto:
20. Jeff Ludes/Alamy: 11b. Monkey
Business Images/Shutterstock: front
cover, 19. David Parsons/istockphoto:
12. David Pearson/Alamy: 25br. Denis
Radovanovic/istockphoto: 15tr. Rada
Razvan/Shutterstock: 14. Alistair Scott/
istockphoto: 9tr. Stephen Strathdee/
istockphoto: 7. Tony Tremblay/
istockphoto: 6. 21 Archive/istockphoto:
27tl. Vibrant Image Studio/Shutterstock:
21b. Peter Vopenka/Shutterstock:
13. H Mark Weldman/Alamy: 17.
Karen Winton/Shutterstock: 11c.
Linda Yolanda/istockphoto: 25t. Yvan /
Shutterstock: 8. Every attempt has been
made to clear copyright. Should there be
any inadvertent omission please
apply to the publisher for rectification.

Contents

KT-211-668

...d out ways to help your planet in this book and become an eco hero like me!

Words in **bold** are in the glossary on page 28.

on the move

Every day, all over the world, we move around in different ways. We walk or ride a bike, but we also travel in vehicles such as cars, buses, trains and planes.

We also use lorries, vans and planes to carry things that we need, such as clothes, toys and food from place to place. Every vehicle needs **fuel** to make it move.

How do you travel around?

Fossil fuels

Most vehicles run on **petrol** or **diesel**. These are made from a **fossil fuel** called **oil**. Fossil fuels are made from plant and animal materials. Fossil fuels take millions and millions of years to form under the ground.

An **oil rig** is used to drill down deep below the sea to find oil.

We are using up fossil fuels very quickly. Once we run out of fossil fuels it will take millions of years for more to form.

Fuel is very important to us. Eco heroes don't waste it!

Using less fuel

There are lots of simple things you and your family can do to save fuel.

Be an eco hero by:

• Helping to empty the car boot. If a car boot is full the car is much heavier. The car has to use more fuel if the car is heavy.

• Opening the window instead of asking to use the air conditioning. Air conditioning uses fuel.

• Reminding adults to check tyre pressures. Having tyres at the right pressure saves fuel.

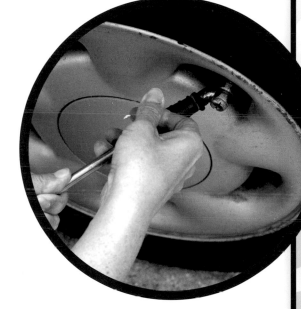

• Helping to take off roof racks and top boxes when you do not need them. A roof rack or top box slows the car down and uses more fuel.

Roof rack

Air pollution

Most vehicles on the road cause **pollution.** As their engines use fuel they make **gases** that can poison the air and cause **global warming.**

Ships, aeroplanes and some trains also pump out gases that are very bad for the planet.

We breathe in these gases and it can be bad for us. Pollution in the air also mixes with rain. This makes **acid rain**, which can damage trees and buildings.

These trees have been killed by acid rain.

Short journeys

Be an eco hero by cutting down car use. For a short journey, such as going to school, try not to travel by car. See if you can find another way to travel and you will:

- save fuel
- cut down pollution
- help to clean the air.

Walk

Scoot

Skateboard

Run

15

Car share

Many people use their cars to travel to work and to school. If you make everyday journeys like this, you could work out a car share **rota**.

Be an eco hero by giving someone a ride or getting one yourself.

If you share a car journey, the car is full rather than carrying just one or two people. This means fewer cars on the road, which causes less pollution. The roads are safer too.

Riding a bike

You can be an eco hero by riding a bike.
This is good for the planet and it is also
good for you.

Riding a bike does not use petrol, does not cause pollution and keeps you fit!

Remember to cycle safely and wear a helmet.

Travel by bus

You are an eco hero if you travel by bus or **tram**. This is a good way to use less fuel and cut down pollution. Travelling by bus or tram means less traffic on the roads. A 30-seater bus can mean 30 fewer cars on the road.

If you go on a day trip, try to find out if you can travel by bus. Travelling on a bus with your friends is fun.

Travel by train

Trains are a fast way to travel around.
Train travel can help save fuel, reduce
traffic and cut down pollution. It can also
be more fun to travel by train.

Travelling on a full train is better than each person travelling in their own car. It cuts down on traffic jams too.

Eco shopping

Every day, lorries, vans, planes and trains **transport** food all over the planet. This makes more traffic, uses fuel and causes pollution.

Be an eco hero by:

- Reading food labels to find out how far your food has travelled and choosing **local** food if you can. The food will be fresher and you will be helping local farmers.
- Helping to do the supermarket shop online.
- Getting toys and clothes delivered to your home.

Choose local food

Shop online

Home delivery

A van delivering to 50 homes means 50 fewer cars on the road.

Eco hero activities

Here are some eco hero activities you could do at home.

Be an eco hero!
Don't travel by car.

Walk, skate, scoot or cycle instead!

Help your friends be eco heroes! Make a poster to show all the ways to get around without causing pollution. You could use pictures from magazines or the Internet.

Ask an adult to help you write a letter to your council asking for more cycle paths and bicycle lanes where you live.

Bicycle lanes make cycling safer.

Learn how your bike works and how to clean and mend it.

Clean bikes last for longer.

Glossary

acid rain   rain that is full of dangerous chemicals.

diesel   a type of fuel.

fossil fuel   materials found deep under the ground and formed over millions of years from dead animals and plants.

fuel   material used to make heat or light, usually by being burned. Coal, gas and oil are types of fuel.

gas   air-like substance that you cannot see.

global warming   worldwide rise in temperatures affecting sea levels and weather.

local   a person, place or shop that is in your neighbourhood.

oil   thick, dark liquid found deep under the ground.

oil rig   a structure used for drilling for oil.

petrol   a type of fuel made from oil.

pollution   gas or liquid that dirties or poisons air or water.

rota   a list of dates and times and who does what.

tram   a vehicle that runs along a fixed track.

transport   to move people or things from place to place.

Learn more

This book shows you some of the ways you can be an eco hero. But there is plenty more you can do to save the planet. Here are some websites that have lots of ideas and information to help you learn more about being an eco hero:

www.foe.co.uk/learning/educators/resource/ index.html#Primary
Friends of the Earth posters packed with information about pollution and climate change.

www.theplanetpatrol.com
Find out all about global warming and the things we can all do to tackle it.

http://tiki.oneworld.net/
Find out about climate change with Tiki the penguin.

www.dingding.org.uk/games/manchester/town/ index.html
Great site with good mix of fun travel games.

Note to parents and teachers: Every effort has been made by the Publishers to ensure that these websites are suitable for children, that they are of the highest educational value, and that they contain no inappropriate or offensive material. However, because of the nature of the Internet, it is impossible to guarantee that the contents of these sites will not be altered. We strongly advise that Internet access is supervised by a responsible adult.

Index